SECRET CODES 3

for

Sony®

PlayStation®

D0884979

||||BradyGAMES
STRATEGY GUIDES

||||BradyGAMES
STRATEGY GUIDES

LEGAL STUFF

SECRET CODES 3 FOR SONY® PLAYSTATION®

Brady Publishing
An Imprint of
Macmillan Digital Publishing USA
201 W. 103rd Street
Indianapolis, Indiana 46290

ISBN: 1-56686-799-1

Library of Congress Catalog No.: 98-071835

Printing Code: The rightmost double-digit number is the year of the book's printing; the rightmost single-digit number is the number of the book's printing. For example, 98-1 indicates that the first printing of the book occurred in 1998.
00 99 98   3 2

Manufactured in the United States of America.

Oddworld: Abe's Oddysee ™ and © 1997 Oddworld Inhabitants, Inc. All rights reserved. Published and distributed by GT Interactive Software Corp.

One™ and ASC Games are trademarks of American Softworks Corporation. One™ is co-developed by Visual Concepts. ©1997 American Softworks Corporation.

PaRappa the Rapper is a trademark of Sony Computer Entertainment America Inc. ©1997 Sony Computer Entertainment Inc. ©Rodney A. Greenblat/Interlink.

Red Asphalt is a trademark of Interplay Productions. All rights reserved.

Resident Evil 2 ©CAPCOM CO., LTD. 1997, 1998 ©CAPCOM U.S.A., INC. 1997, 1998 All rights reserved. Resident Evil is a trademark of CAPCOM CO., LTD. CAPCOM is a registered trademark of CAPCOM CO., LTD.

Shipwreckers™, Psygnosis, and the Psygnosis logo are trademarks of Psygnosis Ltd. ©1997 Psygnosis Ltd. All rights reserved.

Skullmonkeys ©1998 DreamWorks Interactive L.L.C. All rights reserved. Skullmonkeys is a trademark of DreamWorks Interactive L.L.C. DreamWorks Interactive is a trademark of DreamWorks L.L.C. All rights reserved.

Spawn®: The Eternal™ ©1997 Sony Computer Entertainment America Inc. Spawn is a registered trademark and The Eternal is a trademark of Todd McFarlane Productions Inc.

Star Wars: Masters of Teras Kasi ®, ™, and ©1997 Lucasfilm Ltd. All rights reserved.

Street Fighter EX Plus Alpha ©ARIKA CO, LTD 1997. ©CAPCOM USA, INC 1997. All rights reserved. Street Fighter is a trademark of CAPCOM CO., LTD. CAPCOM is a trademark of CAPCOM CO., LTD.

Tekken™3 is a trademark of NAMCO CO., LTD.

Time Crisis is a trademark of NAMCO CO., LTD. All rights reserved.

BRADYGAMES STAFF

Publisher
Lynn Zingraf

Editor-In-Chief
H. Leigh Davis

Title/Licensing Manager
David Waybright

Marketing Manager
Janet Eshenour

Aquisitions Editor
Debra McBride

Marketing Assistant
Ken Schmidt

Credits

Cevelopment Editor
David Cassady

Project Editor
Timothy Fitzpatrick

Screenshot Editor
Michael Owen

Creative Director/Book Designer
Scott Watanabe

Production Designer
Dan Caparo
Dave Eason
Jane Washburne

SECRET CODES 3 FOR SONY® PLAYSTATION®

CONTENTS

SECRET CODES

ACE COMBAT 2 15

AUTO DESTRUCT 15

BEAST WARS 18

BLOODY ROAR 18

BRAVO AIR RACE 20

BUSHIDO BLADE 20

BUSTER BROS. COLLECTION 20

CART WORLD SERIES 21

CASTLEVANIA: SYMPHONY
OF THE NIGHT 23

CLOCK TOWER 24

CODENAME: TENKA 24

COLONY WARS 25

COMMAND & CONQUER:
RED ALERT 26

COOL BOARDERS 2 28

COURIER CRISIS 29

CRASH BANDICOOT 2 30

CRITICAL DEPTH 30

CROC: LEGEND OF THE GOBBOS . . .31

THE CROW: CITY OF ANGELS 32

DARKLIGHT CONFLICT 34

DEAD OR ALIVE 35

DESCENT MAXIMUM 35

DRAGON BALL GT: FINAL BOUT 39

DUKE NUKEM TOTAL MELTDOWN . . .39

DYNASTY WARRIORS 40

EXCALIBUR 2555 AD 41

FELONY 11-79 42

FIFA '98: ROAD TO THE
WORLD CUP 43

FIGHTING FORCE 44

FORMULA 1: CHAMPIONSHIP
EDITION 45

FROGGER 48

G-POLICE 48

GRAN TOURISMO 51

GEX: ENTER THE GECKO 52

HEXEN 53

LOST WORLD: JURASSIC PARK 53

MADDEN NFL '98 55

MARCH MADNESS '98 56

MICRO MACHINES V3 57

MORTAL KOMBAT 4 58

MORTAL KOMBAT MYTHOLOGIES:
SUB-ZERO 61

MOTO RACER 62

NAMCO MUSEUM VOL. 5 65

NASCAR '98 65

NBA IN THE ZONE 2 67

NBA LIVE '98 68

NCAA FOOTBALL '98 72

NCAA GAMEBREAKER '98 73

NEED FOR SPEED III:
HOT PURSUIT 74

NFL GAMEDAY '98 78

NHL '98 80

NHL BREAKAWAY '98 84

NHL FACE OFF '98 87

NIGHTMARE CREATURES 88

ODDWORLD: ABE'S ODDYSEY 89

ONE 91

PANDEMONIUM 2 92

PARAPPA THE RAPPER 94

PEAK PERFORMANCE 95

PITFALL 3D: BEYOND
THE JUNGLE 95

POWERBOAT RACING 99

RED ASPHALT 99

RESIDENT EVIL 2 101

RUSH HOUR 103

SAN FRANCISCO RUSH 104

SHADOW MASTER 105

SHIPWRECKERS 105

SKULLMONKEYS 107

SPAWN: THE ETERNAL 108

STAR WARS:MASTERS
OF TERAS KASI 109

STREET FIGHTER EX PLUS α . . .112

TEKKEN 3 113

TIME CRISIS 115

TOMB RAIDER II 115

TREASURES OF THE DEEP 116

TRIPLE PLAY '99 122

WCW NITRO 125

WING COMMANDER IV:
THE PRICE OF FREEDOM 127

XEVIOUS 3D/G+ 128

CODES LEGEND

ABBREV.	BUTTON
▲	Triangle button
●	Circle button
X	X button
■	Square button
Up	Up on D-pad
Right	Right on D-pad
Down	Down on D-pad
Left	Left on D-pad
R1	R1 button, top of controller
R2	R2 button, top of controller
L1	L1 button, top of controller
L2	L2 button, top of controller

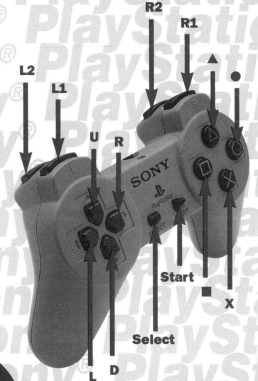

R2

R1

L2

L1

U   R

SONY

Start

■   X

Select

L   D

ACE COMBAT 2

Extra Aircraft Mode
Finish the game and watch the Normal or Bonus Ending. This will make some new aircraft available for sale after finishing certain missions.

Free Mission Mode
Finish the game using the Extra Aircraft Option and watch the Normal or Bonus Ending. You should now be able to play any mission you have seen.

Music Player
Complete the game with a rank higher than First Lieutenant. The music player should appear in the Options Screen.

Viewing Aircraft In 3D
Complete your collection of medals by shooting down the skilled enemy pilots. This option should appear in the Options Screen.

AUTO DESTRUCT

Cheat Menu
Pause the game and press Up, Down, Left, Right, Down, Right, L1, R1, R1.

Now you can enable the following codes:

EFFECT   CODE

Blood Mode	Press L1, Down, R1, Left, L1, Right, R1
Angel Mode	Enable Blood Mode, then press Up, R1, Down, L1, Up, Left, R1, Right, L1.
Extra Time	Press Down, L1, L1, ●, ●, R1, Up, ■, L1
More Cash	Press L1, R1, Up, ●, Down, ■, Left, R1, L1
More Nitros	Press L1, ●, Down, L1, Up, ■, ●, R1
Infinite Fuel	Press L1, ●, Right, L1, ●, R1, L1, Up, R1, Down
Invulnerability	Press L1, L1, L1, L1, Left, ●, ●, ■, L1
Next Mission	Press L1, Right, Down, Left, Up, R1

All Time Trials	Press R1, L1, ●, Left, ●, ●, Right, L1, ●
Mission Select	Press Up, Down, ●, L1, R1, L1, ●, Down, Up
Tune Up Menu	Press L1, R1, L1, Up, Down, ●, Down, Right, Left, ■, R1
Car Select (from Tune Up menu)	Press Left, R1, Right, R1, Left, R1, Right, R1

Debug Mode

Pause the game and press Up, Right, Left, Down, ●, L1, R1, R1, L1, ●, Down, Left, Right, Up.

A B C D E F G H I J K L M N O P Q R S T U V W X Y Z

BEAST WARS

Level Skip

Pause the game, then hold L2 and press Up, Down, Left, Right, ▲, X, X, ▲, Right, Left, Down, up. Continue to hold L2 and unpause.

BLOODY ROAR

Alternate Outfit

You can select a different outfit for your character by pressing ●.

Giant Mode

Hold L2 while you select your character.

Kid Mode
Hold R2 while you select your character.

Large Arena
Defeat 10 opponents in a row in Survival Mode to increase the size of the battle arena.

Life Recovery
Defeat the game with Bakuryu on Level 4 or above to access regenerating life bars.

Larger Arms
Defeat the game with no continues on Level 4 or above.

No Gauge Mode
Defeat the game with Yugo.

No Walls
Defeat the game with Mitsuko without morphing into beast mode.

Alternate Outfit—Alice
Defeat all opponents in Time Attack Mode in under 10 minutes.

A
B
C
D
E
F
G
H
I
J
K
L
M
N
O
P
Q
R
S
T
U
V
W
X
Y
Z

BRAVO AIR RACE

F16 and Stealth Jet

At the Title screen, press and hold R1 + L2 on controller two, and then press the Select button 20 times. You will hear a sound when entered correctly.

BUSHIDO BLADE

Playing as Katze

To play as Katze, you must fight your way through all 100 Slash Mode enemies *without* dying.

BUSTER BROS. COLLECTION

Bonus Levels

In Buster Buddies, start a normal game by pressing X on both controllers.

Level Select

In Super Buster Bros. and Buster Buddies, press Down + X when choosing a normal game.

CART WORLD SERIES

Bonus Cars

At the Create a Driver screen, enter your name as PUSHBUTT.

Bonus Track

At the Create a Driver screen, enter your name as EPILEPTI to access the Titon tracks.

Cheat Codes

To access the following cheats, enter these codes as your name on the Create a Driver screen.

ENTER DRIVER NAME

WHEELS

ABCDEFGHI JKLM
NOPQR TUVWXYZ
DEL SPACE END

× SELECT △ CANCEL

EFFECT	CODE
Half Gravity on Tracks	FLOAT
Three Quarters Gravity	FEATURE
More Gravity on Tracks	RADBRAD
No Collision on Cars	BANZAI

Cars Only Have Wheels　　　　**WHEELS**

Cars Have Fat Tires	**FAT TIRES**
Win Season	**WTFIN**
Invincible In Sim Mode	**IMMORTAL**
Two Laps In Season Mode	**GEK**
Sunset Tracks	**SUNNYSKY**
Night Tracks	**NIGHTRID**
Space Tracks	**SPACERID**

CASTLEVANIA: SYMPHONY OF THE NIGHT

Axe Lord Armor

After beating the game once, start a new game and enter your name as AXEARMOR.

Enhanced Luck

After beating the game once, start a new game and enter your name as X-X!V"Q.

Play as Richter

After beating the game once, start a new game and enter your name as RICHTER.

CLOCK TOWER

Jennifer's Alternate Outfit

Instead of going to Rick's house in the second scenario, use Helen to go to the library in the second scenario. This is accomplished by *not* asking Harris to show the statue to Rick in the first scenario, and making the trip by yourself instead of asking Nolan to help you. When you arrive at the Barrow's Castle in the third scenario, Jennifer will be wearing a different uniform.

CODENAME: TENKA

All Weapons

Pause the game, hold L1 and press ▲, R1, ▲, ■, R1, ●, ■, ■. Then release L1.

Level Warp

Pause the game, hold L2 and press ●, ●, ■, ▲, R1, ■, ▲, ●. Then release L2.

COLONY WARS

Switch All Cheats Off
Enter All*cheats*off as a password.

Select Level
Enter Commander*Jeffer as a password.

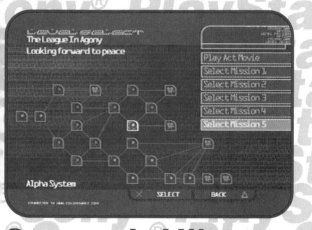

Supercooled Weapons
Enter Tranquillex as a password.

A
B
C
D
E
F
G
H
I
J
K
L
M
N
O
P
Q
R
S
T
U
V
W
X
Y
Z

Infinite Secondary Weapons

Enter Memo*X33RTY as a password.

Infinite Energy

Enter Hestas*Retort as a password.

COMMAND & CONQUER: RED ALERT

To enter the following codes, click on the Teams menu using the Cancel button (● by default). Then move the cursor over the appropriate icons on the menu bar and press the Cancel button on each.

For example, to enter the Atomic Bomb code, move the cursor to the Circle icon, then press Cancel. Repeat this with the remaining symbols, pressing Cancel after each.

Money
■, ■, ●, X, ▲, ●

Nuke
●, X, ●, ▲, ■, ▲, ■

Win Level
X, ■, ■, ●, ▲, ●

Soylent Green
X, ●, ▲, ▲, ●, X

NOTE: This only works in a Skirmish mode.

A
B
C
D
E
F
G
H
I
J
K
L
M
N
O
P
Q
R
S
T
U
V
W
X
Y
Z

COOL BOARDERS 2

Alternate Uniforms

Highlight SBC on the Main menu and press Down, R1, Up, R1, Down, R2, Up, R2, Up, Up, R1, Down, Down, R2. You will hear "Here we go!" each time you press R1 or R2. The new uniforms are available in every mode *except* SBC.

Mirror Mode

Complete SBC, go to the Options screen, and then press Select on the second controller. At the Mode Select screen, press R1 + ■.

Play as the Alien

Score a 38.0 or better in the halfpipe, or complete all 100 moves in Onemake jump.

Play as The Boss

Complete Mirror mode in first place.

Play as the Snowman

Break all the records in Freeride mode.

COURIER CRISIS

To enter the following codes, access the Load/Save Options, select Load, and then choose Password.

Play as an Ape

Enter the password SAVAGEAPES.

Play as an Alien

Enter the password XFIFTYONEX.

CRASH BANDICOOT 2

Extra Lives

To get some extra lives, repeatedly jump up and down on the polar bear in one of the Warp Rooms. You can only do this once per game.

CRITICAL DEPTH

Play As Mr. Phatt

Defeat the game on Medium difficulty.

Play As Agent 326

Defeat the game as Mr. Phatt on Hard difficulty.

Play As Abbadon

Defeat the game as Agent 326 on Hard difficulty.

CROC: LEGEND OF THE GOBBOS

Level Select

To select a level, press Left, Left, Left, Left, Down, Right, Right, Left, Left, Down, Right, Down, Left, Up, Right.

Island Passwords

Level	Password
Island 2	Right, Down, Left, Up, Right, Right, Up, Right, Left, Right, Up, Right, Left, Up, Down

Island 3	Left, Up, Right, Up, Right, Down, Down, Up, Down, Up, Up, Left, Up, Left, Down
Island 4	Right, Down, Down, Up, Right, Left, Up, Right, Down, Up, Up, Right, Left, Up, Down

THE CROW: CITY OF ANGELS

Debug Mode
Enter the password
■, X, ■, ●, ▲, ▲, ●, ■, X, ■

FMV Select
Enter the password
▲, ▲, ●, ●, ●, ●, ●, ●, ▲, ▲

Long Neck Mode
Enter the password
X, ●, ▲, ●, ■, ■, ▲, ●, X, ●

Skinny Mode
Enter the password
▲, ▲, X, ■, ●, ●, ■, X, ▲, ▲

Unlimited Energy
Enter the password
●, X, ▲, X, ●, ▲, ■, ●, X, ■

Passwords

LEVEL	PASSWORD
Pier	▲, X, ▲, ▲, ●, ■, ▲, X, ●
Boat	X, X, X, X, ▲, ■, X, ●
Tomb	▲, ●, ▲, ●, ■, ▲, ▲, ●, X, ●
Grave	X, ▲, X, ▲, ■, X, X, ▲, ■, ●
Church	▲, ▲, ▲, ▲, ●, ■, ▲, ■, ■, ●
Day O' Dead	X, ▲, X, ▲, ■, ●, ●, X, ■, ●
Club	▲, ●, ▲, ●, ●, ▲, X, ●, ■, ●
Tower	X, X, ●, X, ■, ■, X, ▲, ●
Borderland	▲, X, X, X, ●, ■, ▲, ■
Finale	X, X, X, ●, ■, ■, X, X, ▲, ●

DARKLIGHT CONFLICT

Cheat Menu

Go to the Options and enter Down, Down, Up, ■, Left, Left, L1, R1, ●. A new option called Extra should appear on the Main Menu.

Final Level

Enter the password HDVMKXVCK.

DEAD OR ALIVE

Extra Options

After every three hours, an extra option is opened up until five new options have appeared. A clock in the Extra Options Screen keeps the time. After three hours have elapsed on the clock, enter a one player game. When you go back to the title screen, it should say Extra Config open.

DESCENT MAXIMUM

All Accessories
During gameplay, enter
■, ▲, ●, X, X, ▲, ■, X, ●, ■, ●, X

Acid
During gameplay, enter
■, ▲, ●, ■, ▲, ■, X, ▲, X, ▲, ●, X

A
B
C
D
E
F
G
H
I
J
K
L
M
N
O
P
Q
R
S
T
U
V
W
X
Y
Z

All Keys
During gameplay, enter
■, ▲, X, ▲, ●, ▲, X, ▲, X, ▲, ■, X

Toggle Cloak
During gameplay, enter
X, ▲, ●, ■, ●, ▲, ■, X, ▲, X, ▲, ●

Extra Life
During gameplay, enter
▲, X, ■, ●, ▲, X, ■, X, ●, X, ▲, ●

Shields Recharged
During gameplay, enter
▲, X, ●, ■, ■, X, ●, ▲, ■, X, ●, ■

Toggle Robots
Move Fast
During gameplay, enter
▲, X, ■, ■, ▲, ●, ■, X, ●, ■, ▲, ●

Toggle Wingnut
During gameplay, enter
■, ●, ▲, X, ■, ▲, ●, ■, ▲, X, ●

Hello Minnie Message
During gameplay, enter
X, ●, X, ●, X, ●, X, ●, X, ●, X, ●

Mega
Wow/Keys/Levels
During gameplay, enter
▲, ■, ●, X, ▲, ■, ▲, X, ▲, ■, X, ●

Toggle Ten Colors
During gameplay, enter
▲, X, ●, ▲, ■, ●, X, ▲, X, ▲, ●, X

A
B
C
D
E
F
G
H
I
J
K
L
M
N
O
P
Q
R
S
T
U
V
W
X
Y
Z

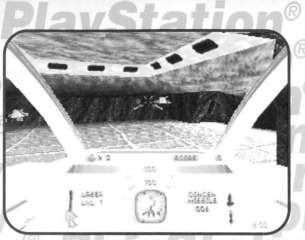

Toggle Turbo

During gameplay, enter
▲, ■, ●, X, ■, X, ●, ■, ▲, ●, X, X

Invulnerability

During gameplay, enter
▲, X, ▲, ●, X, ▲, ■, X, ▲, X, ●, ▲

DRAGON BALL GT: FINAL BOUT

Play as Level 4 Goku

At the Title screen, press **Right, Left, Down, Up, Right, Left, Down, Up.** After entering this, you should hear a tone. Now press ▲ five times and then ■ nine times. When entered correctly, you'll hear another tone and the Menu screen will show a picture of Super Saiyajin Level 4 Goku.

DUKE NUKEM TOTAL MELTDOWN

Quick Health

When in a bathroom, walk up to a toilet and press ▲ (the Action Button). This makes Duke go to the bathroom, and his health goes up 10 points.

Slow Health Revive

To slowly revive your health, shoot a water fountain or fire hydrant, and then stand in the water. While standing in the water, hold the Action Button to slowly revive your health.

A B C **D** E F G H I J K L M N O P Q R S T U V W X Y Z

DYNASTY WARRIORS

Play as Cao Cao

Beat the game with Xiahou Dun, Dian Wei, Xu Zhu, Lu Xun, Taishi, and Diao Chan. To select Cao Cao, move right, off the end of the character selection screen.

Play as Nobunaga

Get three secret characters (Zuge Liang, Lu Bu, Cao Cao). Then, at title screen press Up, ▲, Down, X.

Play as Sun Shang Xiang

Go to the Title Screen, highlight 1P battle, and press Left, Left, Up, Down, ▲, ■, L1, R1.

Play as Toukichi

After getting Cao Cao, press Down, Down, Right, Up, ●, ▲, R1, R2 at the title screen. You should hear a chime if entered correctly.

Play as Zhuge Liang

Beat the game with Zhou Yun, Guan Yu, and Zhang Fei. Then, on your character select screen, press Left, off the end of the character selection screen.

EXCALIBUR 2555 AD

Full Health
Pause the game and press
▲, ▲, ▲, ■, ■, ■, ■, ■

Full Sword Power
Pause the game and press
▲, ▲, ■, ■, ●, ●, ■, ■

Level Skip
Pause the game and press
■, ●, ■, ▲, ●, ▲, ▲, ▲

Passwords

Level	Password
1	●, ■, X ●, ●, ▲
2	■, X ▲, ▲, X ●
3	●, X ●, ▲, ■, X
4	X ●, ▲, ■, ●, ●
5	■, ■, ●, ●, X ▲
6	●, X ■, ▲, ▲, ■

A
B
C
D
E
F
G
H
I
J
K
L
M
N
O
P
Q
R
S
T
U
V
W
X
Y
Z

FELONY 11-79

Secret Cars

To access the secret cars, you need to meet the following conditions:

Car Type	What You Must Do
PCS	Clear the First stage within 4 min.
GTI	Clear the Second Stage within 4 min.
DBL	Clear the Third Stage within 4 min.
VPR	Destroy $1 million on the First Stage and pass the level in the time limit.
ELS	Destroy $2.5 million on the Second Stage and pass the level in the time limit.
360	Destroy $2.5 million in the Third Stage and pass the level in the time limit.
F1	Pass the First Stage with no damage.
PLC	Pass the Second Stage with no damage.
TNK	Pass the Third Stage with no damage.

GTK	Drive through the speed checker on Level 2 at more than 114 mph.
SSP	Drive through the speed checker on Level 2 at more than 144 mph.
RCC	Located in the back-left corner of the mall in Level 3.

FIFA '98: ROAD TO THE WORLD CUP

Easy Money

Enter ■, X, ■, L2, L1 on the Club Transfers screen.

Unlimited Player Attributes

At the Player Edit screen, enter L1, L2, X, ■, X.

A B C D E F G H I J K L M N O P Q R S T U V W X Y Z

FIGHTING FORCE

Invincibility and Level Select

At the Main menu, hold Left + ■ + L1 + R2 until Cheat Mode appears at the bottom of the screen. Then choose Options, where you can enable Invincibility and start on any level.

FORMULA 1: CHAMPIONSHIP EDITION

Cheat Codes

To enable the following codes, enter your name as the following:

Name	Effect
VIRTUALLY VIRTUAL	Virtual reality-style graphics

| **SWAP SHOP** | Background music and new sound effects |
| **LITTLE WHEELZ** | Over-inflated tires |

A
B
C
D
E
F
G
H
I
J
K
L
M
N
O
P
Q
R
S
T
U
V
W
X
Y
Z

PI MAN **Wipeout mode**

ZOOM LENSE **Helicopter viewpoint**

BOX CHATTER   **Murray and Martin sprite commentators**

BILLY BONUS   **Extra tracks**

CATS DOGS	**Rains frogs**
OEAN ALESI	**Round 16 in Championship**
TOO EASY	**First place on all tracks**

FROGGER

Level Select

Pause the game and press Right, ■, ▲, ■, ▲, R1, L1, R1, L1, ●.

Unlimited Lives

Pause the game and press Right, ■, ▲, ■, ▲, X.

G-POLICE

Faster Backup Cars

Enter the password BENIHILL.

Sirens

Enter the password WOOWOO.

Different Camera Angle

Enter the password SUPACAM.

Secret Stages

Enter the password PANTALON.

All Weapons and Unlimited Ammunition

At the Weapons Loadout screen, hold L1 + L2 + R1 + ● + ▲ + ■, and press Left on the D-pad.

Unlimited Shields

At the Briefing screen, hold L1 + R2 + ■ and press Left on the D-pad.

Drive a Car in Training Mode

After finishing the game, return to Training Mode. Then scroll down to the bottom of the menu and select SECRET 3.

Passwords

Mission	Password
2	OLEFGLPI
3	WDZWTYQI
4	STXGIDEA
5	WZKVOFFA
6	GRXJTYGA
7	IMWGTDXI
8	YMPCUZYI
9	YWVFHNAJ
10	WNLUJSBJ
11	UGSIBPNA
12	QEJUXFDJ
13	UGWHVEQA

Mission	Password
14	SFMEZGGJ
15	QSBSSITA
16	WDGSFFJJ
17	USWIQIYA
18	OJFXQEAB
19	QSDHARDB
20	WRRJJDHB
21	ISNEASLB
22	YWGTTQCK
23	YCNHYJEK
24	AUJOMXFK
25	CZHXMGVB
26	EUANLEC
27	EDFIRE
28	STUBOMB
29	THONBOY
30	JIMMAC
31	PUGGER
32	ROSSCO
33	CAKEBOY
34	NIKNAK
35	SAGLORD

GRAN TURISMO

GT Hi-Fi Mode

Win all four races in GT League, and you will get an extra menu in Special Events called GT Hi-Fi. This will give you better sound effects, higher resolution and smoother frame rate by reducing background details.

GEX: ENTER THE GECKO

Cheat Codes

During gameplay, pause the game, and hold L2 or R2 while entering the following cheats:

EFFECT	CODE
Infinite Lives	**UNDEAD**
Invulnerability	**WEASEL**
One Liners	**ALOUD** (Press Select during gameplay)
Rambling GEX	**SENSELESS**
Level Timer	**EARWAX** (At the map, press Select for level stats and press ■ for your best times)

HEXEN

Cheat Menu

At the Options/Pad Config screen, hold R2, and press Right, Down, Right, ▲, X. You should hear a tone if entered correctly. There should be a new option called Cheats on the Main Menu. During gameplay, pause and choose CHEATS.

LOST WORLD: JURASSIC PARK

Character Select

To play as a certain character with 99 lives and all DNA keys, enter the following passwords:

Character	Password
COMPY	X X ● ▲ ■ X ■ X ● ■ ▲ ■
HUNTER	■ ■ ■ ▲ ● X ■ ■ ■ ■ X ● ▲
RAPTOR	X X ● ▲ ■ X ■ X ■ ■ ▲ ●
T-REX	X X ● ▲ ■ ■ ■ X ▲ ■ ▲ ■
PREY	■ ■ ▲ ● X X ■ ■ ▲ X ● ▲

Level Select

At the Password Screen press ■, X, ●, ▲, ▲, X, ■, ●, ▲, ●, X, ■. This must be done three times.

View Galleries

To view the galleries, enter the following passwords:

Gallery	Password
COMPY	X ▲ ▲ ■ X ● ▲ ■ ▲ ● X ●
GENERAL	■ ● ■ ● ● ● ● ■ ● ■ ● ■
HUNTER	▲ X ■ ▲ ● X ■ ● ▲ ■ X ●
PREY	▲ ■ ● ■ X ▲ ▲ ● X ■ ▲ ▲
RAPTOR	● ■ ▲ X ● ▲ ■ X ● ■ X ▲
T-REX	▲ ▲ ● ■ ▲ X ▲ ■ ■ X ▲ ●

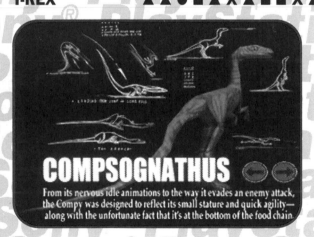

COMPSOGNATHUS

From its nervous idle animations to the way it evades an enemy attack, the Compy was designed to reflect its small stature and quick agility—along with the unfortunate fact that it's at the bottom of the food chain.

MADDEN NFL '98

Bonus Teams

To access one of the bonus teams, select Front Office, and create a player with one of the following names:

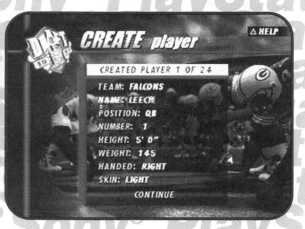

Team	Name
EA Sports Team	ORRS HEROES
Tiburon Team	LOIN CLOTH
All-Time Leaders	LEADERS
All-Time All-Madden	COACH
All 60s Team	PAC ATTACK
All 70s Team	STEELCURTAIN
All 80s Team	GOLD RUSH
NFC	ALOHA
AFC	LUAU

A
B
C
D
E
F
G
H
I
J
K
L
M
N
O
P
Q
R
S
T
U
V
W
X
Y
Z

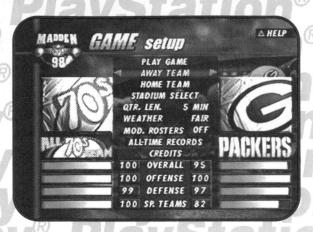

MARCH MADNESS '98

Division One Women's Team

Start a new season, and at the calendar, select Division One at New Mexico. Back out and go into Exhibition Mode screen. The new Division One team should be selectable.

MICRO MACHINES V3

To access the following codes, you must first pause the game and then enter the code. You should hear a sound when entered correctly.

Any Object

Down, Down, Up, Up, Right, Right, Left, Left

Behind Car View

Left, Right, ■, ●, Left, Right, ■, ●

Big Bounces

■, Right, Right, Down, Up, Down, Left, Down, Down

Double Speed

■, X, ●, ■, ▲, X, X, X, X

Slow CPU Cars

●, ▲, ■, X, ●, ▲, ■, X

Debug Mode

Pause the game and press ■, Up, Down, Down, ■, ●, ●, ▲, X to enable Debug Mode. Then press the following during gameplay:

Quit Race and Win	Press Select + X (this doesn't work in time trials)
Change Camera Angle	Hold Select and press Up, Down, Left or Right

| Change Camera Zoom | Hold Select and press L2 or R2. |
| Blow Up All Cars | Hold X + ▲ + ● + ■ |

Other Codes

Enter the following codes as your name. You should hear a sound when entered correctly.

Code	Effect
CATLIVES	9 lives in 1-player mode
GIMMEALL	All tracks in multi-player game
NOTANKS	Tanks cannot shoot
TANKS4ME	Tanks can be used on all tracks except those with water
WINTERY	Slippery roads

MORTAL KOMBAT 4

Hidden Uniforms

To access the character's hidden uniforms and weapons, do the following: At the Select screen, hold down the START button. While holding down the START button, press either the Punch or Kick buttons. Each time you press one of the buttons, your character's picture will spin. Each spin gives you access to one of the new uniform/new weapon combinations. Use this chart to determine which uniform or weapon you will get. Note that some characters DO NOT have new uniforms—instead, they will get different weapons.

CHRACTER	SPIN ONCE	SPIN TWICE	SPIN THREE TIMES
Scorpion	Original Arcade Alternate Uniform	Smoke Uniform + Skull Weapon: Mace Club	Weapon: Curved Blade
Rayden	Original Arcade Alternate Uniform	MK2 Uniform Weapon: Blade Wheel	Weapon: Kali Dagger
Kai	Original Arcade Alternate Uniform	Weapon: Rayden Staff	Biker Gear and Glasses Weapon: Spiked Club
Reptile	Original Arcade Alternate Uniform	MK2 Uniform Weapon:	Weapon: Spike Club
Cage	Original Arcade Alternate Uniform	Weapon: Kali Dagger	Tux Uniform Weapon: Gun
Tanya	Original Arcade Alternate Uniform	Weapon: Ice Wand	Black Dress Uniform Weapon: Hammer
Reiko	Original Arcade Alternate Uniform	Weapon: Dragon Sword	Weapon: Crossbow
Jax	Original Arcade Alternate Uniform	White Outfit Uniform	Weapon: Kali Dagger Weapon: Spear
Jarek	Original Arcade Alternate Uniform	Weapon: Wood Hammer	Weapon: Wood Hammer
Quan Chi	Original Arcade Alternate Uniform	Weapon: Wide Blade Sword	Weapon: Crossbow
Fujin	Original Arcade Alternate Uniform	Weapon: Spiked Club	Weapon: Spear
Sub Zero	Original Arcade Alternate Uniform	Frozen Uniform Weapon: Ax	Weapon: Dragon Sword
Shinnok	Original Arcade Alternate Uniform	Weapon: Broad Sword	Weapon: Boomerang
Liu Kang	Original Arcade Alternate Uniform	Karate Uniform Weapon: Dragon Sword	Weapon: Dragon Sword
Sonya	Original Arcade Alternate Uniform	Weapon: Kali Dagger	Purple Outfit Weapon: Mace Club

A
B
C
D
E
F
G
H
I
J
K
L
M
N
O
P
Q
R
S
T
U
V
W
X
Y
Z

Versus Screen Kodes

Player 1	Player 2	Effect
123	123	One-Hit Win
012	012	Noob Saibot Mode
020	020	Red Rain (only on the Rain stage)
050	050	Explosive Kombat
002	002	Weapon drawn and can't be knocked out of your hands
100	100	Disable Throws
010	010	Disable Max Damage
110	110	No Throw/Disable Max Damage
111	111	Free Weapon (Random weapon falls)
222	222	Start with Random Weapon
333	333	Randper Kombat
444	444	Start with Weapons Drawn
555	555	Many Weapons
666	666	Silent Kombat
321	321	Big Head Mode

Stage Select Kodes

Player 1	Player 2	Stage
011	011	Goro Lair (Spike Pit)
022	022	The Well (Scorpion's Stage)

033	033	Elder God's (Blue Face)
044	044	The Tomb Stage
055	055	The Rain Stage
066	066	Snake Stage
101	101	Shaolin Temple
202	202	Living Forest
303	303	Prison (Fan Stage)
313	313	Ice Pit Level

MORTAL KOMBAT MYTHOLOGIES: SUB-ZERO

Enter the following codes at the Password screen:

Unlimited Urns
NXCVSR

1000 Lives
GTTBHR

View Credits
GRVDTS

A
B
C
D
E
F
G
H
I
J
K
L
M
N
O
P
Q
R
S
T
U
V
W
X
Y
Z

Fight Bosses

ZCHRRY(Transports you to Level 8—Shinnok's Fortress. If you die before reaching a checkpoint, press L1 to fight Quan Chi or L2 to fight Shinnok.)

Fatality Against Scorpion (1st Level) and Kia

Forward, Down, Forward, High Punch

Passwords

Level	Passwords
2	THWMSB
3	CNSZDG
4	ZVRKDM
5	JYPPHD
6	QFTLWN
7	XJKNZT

MOTO RACER

All the following codes must be entered at the Title screen:

Limit CPU to 50 Km/h

Down, Down, Down, ●, L1, ●, L2, Down, Down, X

All Normal Tracks
Up, Up, Left, Right, Down, Down, ●, R2, ▲, X

All Reversed Tracks
Down, Down, Right, Left, Up, Up, ●, L2, ▲, X

Pocket Bikes
Up, Down, R2, L2, Down, Up, L1, X

Night Racing
Up, ●, L1, Down, ▲, L2, ●, Left, R1, X

Reverse Mode
Left, Right, Left, Right, ●, ●, R1, L1, ▲, X

Turbo Boost
Up, Up, Up, ▲, R1, ▲, R2, Up, Up, X

View Credits
● , ▲ , ● , ● , ▲ , ● , Up, Right, Left, X

View Ending
● , ▲ , ● , ▲ , ● , ▲ , L1, Up, R2, X

NAMCO MUSEUM VOL. 5

Raise Vitality for Dragon Buster:

At the Dragon Buster title screen, press **SELECT** ten times, and then start the game. When your vitality drops to 32 or below, press **L1 + R1**. Your vitality will rise to 128 and you will lose one credit.

Grobda Level Select

At the Title Screen, press and hold **L1+L2+R1+R2** and then press Start.

NASCAR '98

Shooter Mode

During a race, pause the game and go to Race Statistics. Then press **R1 + R2 + L1 + L2** and you will hear an engine roar. Continue the race and press ▲ to shoot at your opponents.

A B C D E F G H I J K L M N O P Q R S T U V W X Y Z

Pinnacle Car

In exhibition mode, go to the Race Setup/Car Select screen and highlight the Bobby Labonte car. Then hold X and press Up, Down.

EA Sports Car

In exhibition mode, go to the Race Setup/Car Select screen and highlight the Kenny Wallace car. Then hold X and press Up, Down.

Turbo Mode

At the Options screen, hold ● then press Up, Left, Down, Right.

NBA IN THE ZONE 2

All-Star Team in Exhibition Mode

At the Title screen with the cursor on Start, press and hold L1 + R2 + Select + Start until the screen fades out. This should enable you to select the All-Star Team in Exhibition Mode.

Play As Magic Johnson

To get Magic Johnson, go to the Create a Player option and choose Create a New Player.

Choose model number 25. When you see the player in a game, you should see Magic's face. He will also be wearing knee pads.

Play As Larry Bird

To get Larry Bird, do the same thing you did to get Magic, except choose model number 29.

A
B
C
D
E
F
G
H
I
J
K
L
M
N
O
P
Q
R
S
T
U
V
W
X
Y
Z

NBA LIVE '98

EA Production Teams

Enter the following names at the Custom Teams screen:

EA Europals
Hitmen Coders
Hitmen Earplugs
Hitmen Idlers
Hitmen Pixels
QA Campers
QA Testtubes
TNT Blasters

Easter Eggs

Start a normal game and access the User Setup screen. At the User Setup screen, start a new username and enter Secrets. Press Start to confirm the name. Press ● to uncover the Secrets menu.

To use one of these codes, go to the Secrets menu, highlight ENTER SECRET CODE, and then press X. After entering one of the codes, just press Start. Remember that the codes are *case sensitive*!

Underwater Seaweed Court
Seaweed

Halloween Team (Home Team)
Scary

Halloween Team (Visitor Team)
Freaky

Invisible Team (Home Team)
Cloak home

Invisible Team (Visitor Team)
Cloak away

Player with Eyepatch
Eyepatch

Player with Monocle
Monocle

EA Toque Player
Toque

Prisoners
Prisoners

Chameleon Home Team
Lizard

Chameleon Away Team
Reptile

Pin, the Teddy Bear
Pin rocks

nba live 98 secrets

Enter Secret Code: Pin rocks

You have attempted to activate the 'Pin, the Teddy Bear' feature. You must answer this skill testing question. Is Pin loveable, or adorable?

he's both
he's loveable
he's adorable

A
B
C
D
E
F
G
H
I
J
K
L
M
N
O
P
Q
R
S
T
U
V
W
X
Y
Z

NCAA FOOTBALL '98

Hidden Teams

Select Exhibition, press X at the Team Selection Screen, and press the X button again on the following screen. In the User Records Screen, enter the following passwords. You should hear "It's in the game" if you entered the code correctly.

PASSWORD	TEAM
JEXLAD	'73 Alabama
OEDYIJ	'78 Alabama
WHVCIR	'89 Alabama
ZDDJOT	'92 Alabama
CEVHETS	'89 Colorado
VEWOJ	'96 Florida
MYLQLOH	'93 Florida State
RCIXRE	'96 Florida State
ZOWS	'82 Georgia
EIWQOH	'83 Miami
WEVKIM	'87 Miami
WMIXJ	'89 Miami
WYGGKEP	'91 Miami
ANOYSAJ	'94
BSEPMAJ	'65 Michigan State
KCIZRE	'91 Michigan
IGSI	'83 Nebraska

Code	Team
EGAXRIM	'91 Nebraska
SNXAI	'93 Nebraska
BNOYD	'94 Nebraska
JNIVED	'73 Notre Dame
REGRZOJ	'88 Notre Dame
AGIG	'79 Ohio State
HTOYOMS	'85 Oklahoma
RSGPC	'94 Oregon
IEEIH	'78 Penn State
CCHN	'82 Penn State
HREG	'85 Penn State
AERE	'86 Penn State
LMTE	'65 Penn State
EERC	'68 USC
FSYT	'79 USC
TSTR	'91 Washington
AAYI	West Virginia

NCAA GAMEBREAKER '98

Code	Effect
BEAT DOWN	Make season team all 99s in game
JUMP	Allow to change season team during season
GIMME	Activates all all-time teams

A B C D E F G H I J K L M N O P Q R S T U V W X Y Z

Code	Effect
BUILDER	High attributes in Create Player
Ala 92	Alabama 92
ASU 96	Arizona St. 96
Col 89	Colorado 89
Fla 96	Florida 96
FSU 92	Florida State 92
GB98 Allstars	Game Breaker 98 All Stars
Miami 89	Miami 89
Mich 91	Michigan 91
Neb 95	Nebraska 95
ND 90	Notre Dame 90
OSU 96	Ohio State 96
Okla 79	Oklahoma 79
Penn 78	Penn State 78
W. Vir 88	West Virginia 88

NEED FOR SPEED III: HOT PURSUIT

Cheats

Go to the user name screen in the options menu and enter the following codes:

CODE	EFFECT
MCITYZ	Empire City Bonus Track

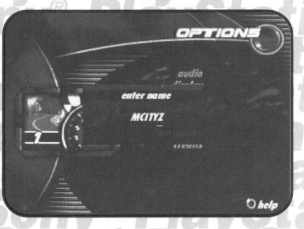

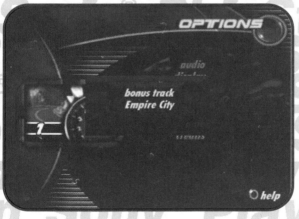

Gldfsh	Scorpio-7 Bonus Track

A
B
C
D
E
F
G
H
I
J
K
L
M
N
O
P
Q
R
S
T
U
V
W
X
Y
Z

MNBEAM	**Space Race Bonus Track**
XCNTRY	**AutoCross Bonus Track**
XCAV8	**Caverns Bonus Track**
PLAYTM	**The Room Bonus Track**

1JAGX	**Jaguar XJR-15 Bonus Car**
AMGMRC	**Mercedes CLK-GTR Bonus Car**

ROCKET   El Nino Bonus Car

SEEALL   All Camera Views (Access in Options/Cameras)

SPOILT   All Cars and Tracks except the Hidden Tracks

NFL GAMEDAY '98

Easter Eggs

Choose Easter Eggs at the Options screen to enter the following codes:

Code	Effect
JUICE	Players move quickly when desperate
HUMONGOUS	Large players
HORSEMAN	No heads
CREDITS	View credits
LOUD MOUTH	Loud commentator
LEECH	Tighter coverage
HATCHET	Forearm shiver juiced
NYSE	Swim move is juiced
REJECTION	Defensive players jump higher
TOAST	Secondary plays farther off receivers
GLOVES	Better receiving
BETTIS	Fans cheer if you're the Steelers at Pittsburgh
FIRE DRILL	Fast players
LOOK MA	No hands
BLIND REF	No penalties

QUIET CROWD	Quiet fans
EQUAL TEAMS	Teams have equal abilities
SHOW OFF	Dive, then press Jump to perform a roll, and then keep running
VIRTUAL POLYGONS	Flat players
FLEA CIRCUS	Small players
CPU DEFENSE	Better computer defense
CPU OFFENSE	Better computer offense
GD CHALLENGE	Computer plays better
WATERY AI	Stupid computer
BIG FOOT	Long field goals
THIN AIR	Long field goals
AIR STRIKE	More accurate QB

Hidden Teams

When playing as Player 1, press Up on the D-pad to pick a Super Bowl team. If you want an All-Star team, push Up on the D-pad again at the Player Selection screen, and scroll through by pushing L1 and L2.

When playing as Player 2, push Down on the D-pad to get to the Super Bowl teams. Press Down on the D-pad again to access the All-Star teams. Scroll through the teams by pressing R1 and R2.

A B C D E F G H I J K L M N O P Q R S T U V W X Y Z

NHL '98

Cheat Codes

Enter the following codes at the password screen:

Code	Effect
STANLEY	View winning movie
GIPTEA	Faster players
NHLKIDS	Tiny players

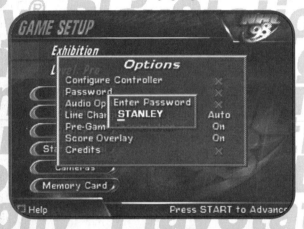

PLAYTIME

Tiny players with normal heads and large goalies

BIGBIG   Huge players
BRAINY   Big heads

A
B
C
D
E
F
G
H
I
J
K
L
M
N
O
P
Q
R
S
T
U
V
W
X
Y
Z

EAEAO   **EA Blades team**

3RD   **Third jersey (if available)**

REEEA   **Adds Developers to the free agent list**

NHL BREAKAWAY '98

Alternate Uniforms

After pressing Start Game on the Setup screen, press Right + ■ until the rink appears. This only works for visiting teams that have three jerseys. Those teams are Anaheim, Boston, Chicago, Tampa Bay, and the N.Y. Rangers.

Cheat Menus

Pause the game and press R1, R2, Right, Left, R1. Go to Statistics to access Pat's Cheats and Pete's Cheats.

Developer Teams

The following will only work in Exhibition or Practice Modes.

When selecting your teams, press L1, L2, ■. The New York Sports, Salt Lake Frosties, and the Canton, MI Ratpack will appear at the beginning of the list.

Extra Teams

The following will only work in Exhibition or Practice Modes.

For the following teams, highlight the team that you want and enter the following codes. Your players will wear the corresponding teams jerseys.

Team	Code
Cleveland Barons	R1, R1, Circle
Toronto St. Pats	L1, L1, Circle
Oakland Seals	L2, L2, Circle
Kansas City Scouts	R2, R2, Square
Montreal Maroons	L1, R1, Square
Portland Rosebuds	L2, R2, Square
Vancouver Millionaires	R2, L2, Circle
New York Americans	R1, L2, Circle
Hamilton Tigers	L1, R2, Square
Seattle Metropolitans	L2, R1, Square

NHL FACE OFF '98

Bonus Players

Go to the Create Player screen and enter one of the following names:

Raja Altenhoff
Tom Braski
Craig Broadbooks
Josh Hassin
Tawn Kramer
Alan Scales
Kelly Ryan
Chris Whaley
Peter Dille
Craig Ostrander

Be sure not to change any of the attributes.

A
B
C
D
E
F
G
H
I
J
K
L
M
N
O
P
Q
R
S
T
U
V
W
X
Y
Z

NIGHTMARE CREATURES

Cheat Mode

At the Password screen, press Up, X, ■, Down, ▲, ■, Down. When you start the game, you will have a Level Select, an Unlimited option, and a Play as Monster option.

Passwords

Level	Password
2	▲, ●, ●, ▲, ▲, Up, X, Up
3	▲, X, ●, Up, ▲, ▲, ■, Left
4	▲, ■, ●, Up, ▲, ●, Up, Left
5	▲, Up, ●, Up, ▲, X, Down, Left
6	▲, Down, ●, X, ▲, X, Left, Down
7	▲, Left, ●, Left, ▲, Down, ▲, ▲

Level	Password
8	▲, Right, ●, Up, ▲, Down, ●, Left
9	●, ▲, ●, ▲, ●, Up, ■, Down
10	●, ●, ●, X, ●, Left, Up, Left
11	●, X, ●, Up, ●, ●, Down, ▲
12	●, ■, ▲, Up, ●, Down, Left, ■
13	●, Up, ▲, X, ●, Down, ▲, X
14	●, Down, ▲, Up, ●, ▲, ●, ■
15	●, Left, ▲, Down, ▲, ●, ■, Up
16	●, Right, ▲, ■, ▲, ●, Up, ■
17	X, ▲, ▲, ■, ▲, X, Down, ■
18	X, ●, ▲, ■, ▲, ■, Left, ■
19	X, X, ▲, Down, ▲, Down, ▲, Up
20	X, ■, ▲, ■, ▲, Down, ●, ■

ODDWORLD: ABE'S ODDYSEY

Green Gas Fart

During gameplay, hold R1, then press Up, Left, Right, ■, ●, X. You need to look closely; it's tough to see.

Level Select

At the Main menu, hold R1 and press Down, Right, Left, Right, ■, ●, ■, ▲, ●, ■, Right, Left.

Movie Select

At the Main menu, hold R1 and press Up, Left, Right, ■, ●, ▲, ■, Right, Left, Up, Right.

ONE

All Weapons
Enter the password Maxpower.

```
                    Load Game

  ▶Enter Password
    Exit




               All weapons selectable
               Press ✕ to enter password
```

Stage Select
Enter the password Hevyfeet.

```
                  Stage Select

    Stage 1 - Opening
    Stage 2 - Metropolis
    Stage 3 - Mountain Fortress
    Stage 4 - Monorail
    Stage 5 - Laboratory
   ▶Stage 6 - Undersea Facility

    Exit
```

A
B
C
D
E
F
G
H
I
J
K
L
M
N
O
P
Q
R
S
T
U
V
W
X
Y
Z

Debug Menu

Enter the password Heybuddy.

Debug Menu

Stage	6
-Section	149
Invincibility	On
All weapons selectable	On
Pause text	Off

Passwords

Stage	Password
2	DIYGIXRA
3	KCSVJTJB
4	RWLKLPBC
5	YQFZMLTC
6	FLZNOHLD

PANDEMONIUM 2

To get some really cool codes, enter the following passwords at the Password screen:

Code	Effect
GETACCES	**Access All Levels**
SKATBORD	**Speed Greed**
HORMONES	**Full Health**

IMMORTAL	**31 Lives**
MAKMYDAY	**Permanent Weapon**
NEVERDIE	**Invulnerable**
GENETICS	**Mutant**

JUSTKIDN   Enemies Regenerate

PARAPPA THE RAPPER

Best Ending

Finish each level with a "Cool" rating, and you'll get a new level where you get to watch Sunny Funny and Katy Kat dance on a table.

You can change the view by pressing the D-pad. You can zoom in and out by pressing R1 and L1. You can change Sunny's and Katy's clothes by pressing the X and ▲ buttons.

PEAK PERFORMANCE

Extra Cars

This cheat works for 1-Player, Time Trial, or the Course Editor modes. To access the extra cars, choose the Car Select menu. Move your cursor to Garage A, and then hold L1 + ●. Now move to Garage B and hold L1 + ● again. Finally, go to Garage C and hold L1 + R1, and press ● again.

PITFALL 3D: BEYOND THE JUNGLE

Original Pitfall

Enter the password CRANESBABY. While playing, press the following:

A
B
C
D
E
F
G
H
I
J
K
L
M
N
O
P
Q
R
S
T
U
V
W
X
Y
Z

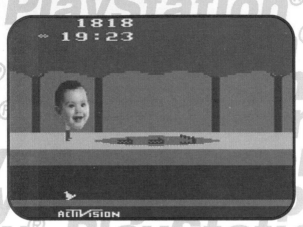

CODE	EFFECT
R1 + R2	Toggles Gary head
R1 + ●	Toggles baby head
R1 + ▲	When a crocodile is on the screen, the one on the far right will say "Hi Mom"
L1 + L2	Toggles infinite lives

Credits
Enter the password CREDITS.

10 Extra Lives
Enter the password GIVEMELIFE.

2-Dimensional Harry
Enter the password 2DHARRY.

Play as Harry in Zero Gravity
Enter the password ZEROGHARRY.

99 Lives
Enter the password **STEVECRANEME**

Turn Off Harry
Commentary
Enter the password **STOPTALKING**

View Comic-style
Cut-scenes
Enter the password **PITFALLCOMIC**

View Cut-scenes
Enter the password PLAYMOVIES

Level Select

Password	Level
CAKEWALK	Level 1
METROPOLIS	Level 2
DEEPDARK	Level 3
TEMPLEME	Level 4
HOTROCKS	Level 5
GOINGDOWN	Level 6
WOWTHATSHOT	Level 7
JAILBREAK	Level 8
THUNDERDOMES	Level 9
MAGICGARDEN	Level 10
SPOOKYMESAS	Level 11
GEEHEISBIG	Boss 1
BIGWORMGUY	Boss 2
BESTFORLAST	Boss 3

POWERBOAT RACING

Big Engines

Enter your name as LARGE in Challenge Mode.

Faster Boats

Enter your name as ZOOOOOM or SPEEEED in Challenge Mode.

Huge Heads

Enter your name as DEFORM in Challenge Mode.

RED ASPHALT

To enter the following codes, pause the game and then enter the code.

Invincibility

Hold R1 and R2 and then press Up, Left, Right, Down, ▲, ■, ●, X

Infinite Weapons

Hold R1 and R2 and then press Left, Up, Right, Down, ■, ▲, ●, X.
To access the following codes, you must enter them at the Main menu screen. You'll hear a noise when the code is entered correctly.

Play As Boss Cars

Hold L2 and then press Left, Right, Down, Up, ■, ●, X, ▲

A B C D E F G H I J K L M N O P Q R S T U V W X Y Z

Big Cars
Hold R2 + L2 and press Up, Up, Up, ■, ■

Unlimited Cash
Hold L2 and R2 and press Left, Left, Right, Right, ■, ■, ●, ●

RESIDENT EVIL 2

Playing As Hunk

To play as Hunk, you must get an "A" ranking on either second scenario. After defeating the game, you're given the option to save a game with a normal character. You're also given a chance to save a game featuring "another scenario," which features Hunk.

Playing As Tofu

To play as Tofu, you must defeat six scenarios (three complete games) in a row. Plus, you need to obtain Hunk during this process. To break it down, you need to defeat a first scenario, then the second one, then the first scenario again, then the second again, then the first scenario again, and finally the second scenario.

Secret Bonus Weapons

At the end of the game, you get evaluated on your performance. The game scores you on several key factors, such as how long it takes you to finish the game, and how many saves you use.

If you achieve an overall ranking of "A," then you are presented with one of the following weapons:

A Rocket Launcher

Or

A combo Submachine Gun/Gatling Gun

To use your new weapon, you must do the following: At the start of your next game, after getting "graded" on your performance, go to an Item Box and you'll find your bonus weapon already there. After you've received one of these bonus weapons, you can play through the other character's game to get the other one.

You should only use these weapons when you're just fooling around. If you use them during your actual game, you will get major points deducted from your score at the end, and your ranking will drop.

Alternate Costumes

To get an alternate costume, you first need to defeat one of the character's "B" games while getting a high ranking (like an "A" or a "B").

At the conclusion of the ending, you will see a still screen showing you the alley outside of the Police Station and a type of Zombie that you've never seen before.

Also, you will see a message that tells you to rush to the Police Station without picking up any items.

Now you must start the next game and make it to the Police Station without picking up any items.

When you get to the area outside of the Station, check the alley to ensure that the "special" Zombie is there. Then you need to go inside the building, find an Item Box, and grab one of those fancy Bonus Weapons with unlimited ammo. Then, go back outside to the alley and blast the Zombie.

When the Zombie is history, check his body to find the "Special Key." Take the key to the Dark Room, where you develop pictures. There is a set of lockers just to the left of the door. Use the key to open the doors to get the Alternate Costumes!

RUSH HOUR

Hidden Track

At the Title Screen, enter X, Up, ▲, Down, R1, L1. You should hear a chime if entered correctly.

High Performance Cars

At the Title Screen, enter Up, Left, Right, X, ●, ■. You should hear a chime if entered correctly.

Reverse Tracks

At the Title Screen, enter Left, ▲, R1, ●, L1, Down. You should hear a chime if entered correctly.

Super Championship

At the Title Screen, enter Right, ■, Left, ●, Up, X. You should hear a chime if entered correctly.

A
B
C
D
E
F
G
H
I
J
K
L
M
N
O
P
Q
R
S
T
U
V
W
X
Y
Z

SAN FRANCISCO RUSH

Drive the UFO

At the Car Select Screen, hold R1+R2+L1+L2; at the transmission screen press X; then hold ▲ until the race, and you should have the UFO.

After selecting your vehicle, hold L1 until the race begins for a miniature truck or hold R1 for a European vehicle.

SHADOW MASTER

All Weapons

At the beginning of the first level, go forward to the first door that opens and kill the two aliens. Inside the room, press L1 + L2 + R1 + R2 + ●. A red light should come on if you've entered the code correctly.

SHIPWRECKERS

Passwords

Level	Password
1-2	Ship, Skull, Fish, Anchor, Ship, Anchor
1-3	Ship, Anchor, Skull, Ship, Anchor, Fish
1-4	Skull, Ship, Fish, Anchor, Anchor, Ship
2-1	Fish, Fish, Anchor, Ship, Skull, Anchor
2-2	Skull, Anchor, Anchor, Fish, Anchor, Ship
2-3	Fish, Anchor, Ship, Ship, Ship, Skull
2-4	Anchor, Fish, Ship, Skull, Skull, Fish
3-1	Ship, Skull, Skull, Fish, Anchor, Skull
3-2	Fish, Skull, Anchor, Fish, Skull, Fish
3-3	Fish, Fish, Ship, Skull, Fish, Ship

3-4	Ship, Anchor, Ship, Fish, Anchor, Fish
4-1	Skull, Skull, Anchor, Ship, Fish, Fish
4-2	Ship, Anchor, Skull, Fish, Fish, Anchor
4-3	Skull, Ship, Skull, Skull, Fish, Ship
4-4	Ship, Fish, Ship, Fish, Ship, Anchor
5-1	Anchor, Ship, Fish, Skull, Fish, Ship
5-2	Fish, Ship, Anchor, Skull, Ship, Fish
5-3	Ship, Fish, Skull, Anchor, Anchor, Skull
5-4	Skull, Ship, Anchor, Fish, Ship, Skull

Starting Region 5, Level 4

SKULLMONKEYS

Free Halos
Pause the game and press R2, ●, ●, Down, Left, ●, Right, Down

Maximum Lives
Pause the game and press L1, ▲, Down, Left, ●, Select, ■, Right

Passwords

Level	Password
World 2	R2, R2, ●, ■
World 3	R2, ■, R2, R1, ■, X, R1, X, X, R1, ▲
World 4	●, ▲, ■, ▲, ●, R1, R1, L1, X, R1, ■
World 5	L1, L1, ■, L1, ■, R1, ■, L1, ■
World 6	■, R1, L2, X, ▲, X, ●, L1, ■, X, ■, X
World 7	■, R1, ●, L1, ●, R1, ●, L1, X, X, ■, R2
World 8	■, L2, R1, ▲, ▲, X, ■, L1, ■, R1
World 9	R2, ●, R1, R1, ●, X, ●, L1, ■, ▲, ■, L1
World 10	X, L2, ■, ▲, ●, R1, ●, L2, ■, ▲, L1
World 11	R1, X, X, L1, L1, R1, ▲, L1, L2, R1, L2
World 12	L1, L2, ●, L1, R2, R2, R1, L2, L2, R1, ■, L2
World 13	●, ■, X, R2, ●, R1, L2, L1, R2, ■, ▲
World 14	■, L1, L1, R1, R2, ▲, R1, L2, L1, R2, ■, R2
World 15	R2, X, L2, ▲, ▲, L2, R1, R2, L1, R2, L2
World 16	L2, R2, R2, T, T, L2, R1, R2, L1, R2, L1
World 17	X, ▲, R1, L1, R2, L1, R2, L2, L1, R2, ▲, X

A B C D E F G H I J K L M N O P Q R S T U V W X Y Z

SPAWN: THE ETERNAL

Invisibility
Pause the game, hold L1+R1 and press
■, , ●, ●, ▲, X

Invincibility
Pause the game, hold L1+R1 and press
▲, , X, X, ■, ●

All Power-ups
Pause the game, hold L2+R2 and press
▲, , ■, X, ▲, X

All Inventory
Pause the game, hold L2+R2 and press
X, , ●, ▲, ■, ●

Reset Physical
Pause the game, hold L1+R1 and press
X, , ▲, ■, X, ●

Reset Magic
Pause the game, hold L1+R1 and press
▲, , X, ■, ▲, ●

Level Skip
Pause the game, hold L1+R1+L2+R2 and
press ▲, X, ■, ●, ●, ●

STAR WARS: MASTERS OF TERAS KASI

To access any of the hidden characters, the Player Change At Continue option must be set to "No."

Big Head Mode

Press and hold Select while choosing a character. Release Select when the fight begins to get big heads.

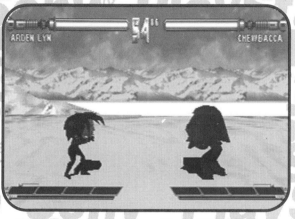

Super Deformed

Press and hold Select, then press Down + X while the game loads.

A
B
C
D
E
F
G
H
I
J
K
L
M
N
O
P
Q
R
S
T
U
V
W
X
Y
Z

Tiny Mode

Press and hold Select + Down + X + R2 while the game loads.

Change Uniforms

Press L1 at the Character Select screen.

Clean Screen

To make the power bars and the force bars disappear, press L1 + R2 + Select while the match is loading.

Invisible Lightsaber

When you pick Luke or Mara Jade, throw the lightsaber that has the super gold power bar. While the lightsaber is in the air, press R2 twice so you can see the handle on Luke or Mara's leg. When the lightsaber returns, it will be invisible unless you move or attack.

Level Select

To access level select on VS. Mode, defeat the game using Chewbacca.

Play As a Stormtrooper

Set the Player Change at Continue option to "No," then defeat the game with Han Solo on the Jedi setting.

Play As Darth Vader

Set the Player Change at Continue option to "No," then defeat the game with Luke Skywalker on the Jedi setting.

Play As Jodo Kast

Play the Survival Mode and defeat all 10 fighters.

Play As Mara Jade

Press and hold L1 + L2 + R1 as you enter the Team Battle Mode. Also, make sure the setting is on Jedi and the Character Change at Continue option is turned off.

BATTLE FOR
MARA JADE

A
B
C
D
E
F
G
H
I
J
K
L
M
N
O
P
Q
R
S
T
U
V
W
X
Y
Z

When done correctly, the computer automatically selects fighters for you, and the words "Battle for Mara Jade" should appear on-screen. Defeat the computer and she will be at your control.

Play As Slave Leia

Defeat the Arcade Mode on the Jedi difficulty setting using Princess Leia. This unlocks Leia's slave outfit.

Fast Credits

When the game credits appear, press and hold Down on the D-pad. This makes the credits go faster. You can also press and hold Up on the D-pad to scroll through the previous credits.

STREET FIGHTER EX PLUS α

Bonus Game

Go to Practice mode, then press Start and press Up, Up, Right, Up, Right, Up, and then Start again. You should see the message "Here comes a bonus game." Enter Practice mode, and the new mode will become available.

TEKKEN 3

Access Characters

Each time you beat the game in Arcade Mode, you'll gain access to a new character. You *must* use a *different character* each time you beat the game in order to access the next new character. Following is the order in which the new characters are revealed:

Beat the Game	Character Revealed
1 Time	Kuma/Panda
2 Times	Julia
3 Times	Gun Jack
4 Times	Mokujin
5 Times	Anna
6 Times	Bryan
7 Times	Heihachi
8 Times	Ogre
9 Times	True Ogre

Alternate Costumes

To access alternate costumes, you must select each of the players in the table the number of times indicated. Play in Arcade, Versus, Force, Team Battle, Time Attack, or Survival modes for your fights. It does not matter weather you win or lose.

Character	Number of Fights
Jin	50
Ling	50
Anna	25
Jack	10

Once you've completed the required fights in the table, select an alternate costume by highlighting a character and pressing Start.

Theater Mode

In Arcade mode, beat the game with each of the ten default characters to gain access to Theater mode.

To access the Sound and Disc options in Full Theater mode, beat the game with every character except Dr. B. and True Ogre.

Tekken Ball Mode

To gain access to Tekken Ball mode, beat the game with nine different characters in Arcade mode.

Gun Jack's Alternate Ending

After releasing Gun Jack's hidden costume, beat the game while using the hidden costume.

Access Dr. B.

Beat the game in Force mode four times to gain access to Dr. B.

Access Gon

Beat the game in Tekken Ball mode once to access Gon.

Access Tiger

Beat the game in Arcade mode with 16 different characters to unlock Tiger. To select Tiger, put the cursor over Eddy and press Start.

TIME CRISIS

Cheat Menu

At the Main menu, shoot the center of the "R" twice, then shoot the center of the target right above the "S" twice. When done correctly, you can increase your lives to nine, adjust your continues, and access unlimited ammo.

TOMB RAIDER II

All Weapons

During gameplay, side step Left, side step Right, side step Left. Walk a step backward, then forward, and spin around three complete times in either direction. Then jump backward and immediately press the Roll button (default ●).

Now press Select to access your inventory.
When done correctly, you should have all
the guns available.

Level Skip

During gameplay, side step Left, side step
Right, side step Left. Walk a step backward, then forward, and spin around three
complete times in either direction. Then
jump forward and immediately press the
Roll button (default ●). When done correctly, you should skip to the end of the level.

Exploding Lara

During gameplay, side step Left, side step
Right, side step Left. Walk a step forward,
then backward, and spin around three complete times in either direction. Then jump
backward or forward and immediately
press the Roll button (default ●).
When done correctly, Lara explodes into
pieces and you have to start your game
over.

TREASURES OF
THE DEEP

You must first pause the game before
entering any of the following codes.

All Equipment

Down, X, Left, ■, Up, Up, ▲, ▲, Right,
Right, ●, ●, L1, L1, L1, L1, R1, R1, R1,
R1, L2, L2, L2, L2, R2, R2, R2, R2

All Missions Available

Down, X, Left, ■, Up, Up, ▲, ▲, Right, Right, ●, ●, Down, Right, Up, Left, ▲, X

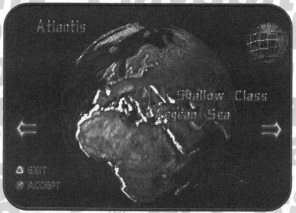

All Missions Complete

Down, X, Left, ■, Up, Up, ▲, ▲, Right, Right, ●, ●, ■, X, X, X, ■, ▲, ▲, ▲, ■, X, X, X

All Weapons

Down, X, Left, ■, Up, Up, ▲, ▲, Right, Right, ●, ●, R1, R1, R1, R1, L1, L1, L1, L1, R2, R2, R2, R2, L2, L2, L2, L2

Banana Bombs

Down, X, Left, ■, Up, Up, ▲, ▲, Right, Right, ●, ●, X, Up, ▲, Down

Complete Current Mission

Down, X, Left, ■, Up, Up, ▲, ▲, Right, Right, ●, ●, ▲, ▲, ▲, Down, Down, Down

A
B
C
D
E
F
G
H
I
J
K
L
M
N
O
P
Q
R
S
T
U
V
W
X
Y
Z

Double Time on Shark Attack

Down, X, Left, ■, Up, Up, ▲, ▲, Right, Right, ●, ●, L2, L2, L2, R1, R1, R1, R2, L1

Extra Continues

Down, X, Left, ■, Up, Up, ▲, ▲, Right, Right, ●, ●, R2, R2, R2, L2, L2, L2

Extra Gold

Down, X, Left, ■, Up, Up, ▲, ▲, Right, Right, ●, ●, R1, R2, L1, L2, R1, R2, L1, L2

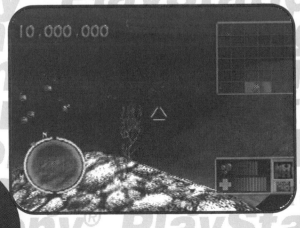

Get Tablet Piece
Down, X, Left, ■, Up, Up, ▲, ▲, Right, Right, ●, ●, L1, L2, L1, L2, ■, ●

Hunting License (No Fines)
Down, X, Left, ■, Up, Up, ▲, ▲, Right, Right, ●, ●, R2, R1, L2, L1

Infinite Air
Down, X, Left, ■, Up, Up, ▲, ▲, Right, Right, ●, ●, ▲, ●, X, ■, Up, Right, Down, Left

Infinite Health
Down, X, Left, ■, Up, Up, ▲, ▲, Right, Right, ●, ●, ▲, ▲, X

No Currents
Down, X, Left, ■, Up, Up, ▲, ▲, Right, Right, ●, ●, R1, L1, L2, R2, X

Open All Doors
Down, X, Left, ■, Up, Up, ▲, ▲, Right, Right, ●, ●, X, ●, ▲, ■

Overhead Camera
Down, X, Left, ■, Up, Up, ▲, ▲, Right, Right, ●, ●, ▲, ■, X, ■. You can zoom in and out by holding Select and pressing L1 or R1

A
B
C
D
E
F
G
H
I
J
K
L
M
N
O
P
Q
R
S
T
U
V
W
X
Y
Z

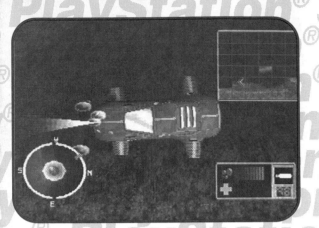

Pass Through Objects

Down, X, Left, ■, Up, Up, ▲, ▲, Right, Right, ●, ●, ■, ■, ●, ●. You can re-enter the code to turn it off.

Refill Air and Health

Down, X, Left, ■, Up, Up, ▲, ▲, Right, Right, ●, ●, Up, Down, Left, Right, X, X

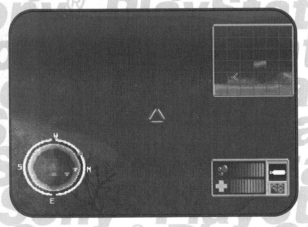

Reveal Entire Map

Down, X, Left, ■, Up, Up, ▲, ▲, Right, Right, ●, ●, ■, X, ●, X, ■

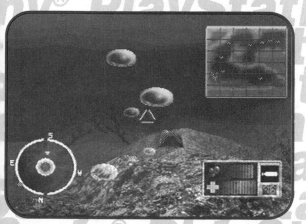

Super Speed

Down, X, Left, ■, Up, Up, ▲, ▲, Right, Right, ●, ●, R1, R2, R1, R2, R1, R2

Turn Off Crosshairs and Information Panels

Down, X, Left, ■, Up, Up, ▲, ▲, Right, Right, ●, ●, ▲, X, Up, Down

Unlimited Payload

Down, X, Left, ■, Up, Up, ▲, ▲, Right, Right, ●, ●, ▲, Up, X, Down

A
B
C
D
E
F
G
H
I
J
K
L
M
N
O
P
Q
R
S
T
U
V
W
X
Y
Z

TRIPLE PLAY '99

Crowd and Announcer Control

To control the crowd noise and the announcer's comments, hold L1+L2+R1+R2 and then enter one of the following codes below:

Crowd Noise

Code	Noise
X, Down, Down, X	Awww!
■, Left, Left, ■	Loud roar
●, Right, Right, ●	Boo

Announcer Comments

Code	Comment
Up,▲,Right,●	Story from Buck
Down,X,Right,●	Facts/Baseball Trivia
Left,■,Right,●	Commercials
●,Right,■,Left	The Nickname Game
X,Down,▲,Up	Weather
Left,■,Up,▲	Display Random Stat

Shout Outs to Game Developers

While holding down L1+L2+R1+R2, press Up, ▲, Up followed by:

CODE	NAME
▲	Jon Spencer
●	Gary Lam
■	Steve Rechtschaffner
X	Chuck Osieja
Up	Brent Nielsen
Left	Pauline Moller
Down	Agathat Kuzniak
Right	Mike "Swanny" Swanson

While holding down L1+L2+R1+R2, press Left, ■, Left followed by:

CODE	NAME
▲	Duncan Lee
●	Yanick Lebel
■	Anne Geiger
X	Edwin Gomez
Up	Wendell Harlow
Left	Stephen Gagno-Cody
Down	Vanessa Gonwick
Right	Adrienne Travica

A B C D E F G H I J K L M N O P Q R S T U V W X Y Z

While holding down L1+L2+R1+R2, press Right, ●, Right followed by:

CODE	NAME
▲	Frank Faugno
●	Michael J. Sokyrka
■	Kirby Leung
X	Jeff Coates
Up	Mike Sheath
Left	Mark Liljefors
Down	Anne Fouron
Right	Kenneth Newby

While holding down L1+L2+R1+R2, press Down, ▲, Down followed by:

CODE	NAME
▲	Carolyn Cudmore
X	Rick Falck
Up	Louis Wang
Left	Mark Dobratz
Down	Brett Marshall
Right	Jason Lee

While holding down L1+L2+R1+R2, press the following:

CODE	NAME
Up four times	Jen Cleary
Left four times	Bob Silliker
Down four times	Eric Kiss
Right four times	Darron Stone

X four times	Ryan Pearson
● four times	Stan Tung
■ four times	Rob Anderson
▲ four times	Mike Rayner

Hidden Stadiums

At the stadium select screen, press
L2, L1, R1, L1, R2.

WCW NITRO

Big Heads

At the Mode Select screen, press R1,
R1, R1, R1, R1, R1, R1, R2, Select.

Ring Select

At the Options menu, press R1, R2, R1, R2, Select. Then press the Select button to cycle through the rings.

Swelled Head

At the Character Select screen, press L1, L1, L1, L1, L1, L1, L1, L2, Select. Each time you get hit or hit your opponent, your character's head gets bigger.

Hidden Characters

At the Title screen, press R1, R1, R1, R1, L1, L1, L1, L1, R2, R2, R2, R2, L2, L2, L2, L2, Select. You should a sound when entered correctly.

WING COMMANDER IV: THE PRICE OF FREEDOM

Level Select

At the copyright screen, press Up, Down, Down, Up, R2. Use R1 and R2 to select the Scene.

One Shot Kill

Press L1 + L2 + ■ to eliminate your target.

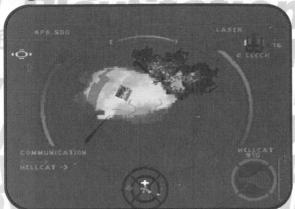

XEVIOUS 3D/G+

Play as Heihachi

At title screen, hold X + Left + ●+ Start until the game begins.

Play as the Black Ship

At the title screen, move the cursor to the Reset option, and hold L1 + L2 + R1 + R2. Press Start while still holding the top buttons until your ship changes color.

Unlimited Continues

At the game selection screen hold L1 + R1 + L2 + R2 and press Circle.